CPS

Centre for Policy Studies

WHAT ARE SPECIAL EDUCATIONAL NEEDS?

AN ANALYSIS OF A NEW GROWTH INDUSTRY

Dr John Marks

Why, sometimes I've believed as many as six impossible things before breakfast – The White Queen in *Through the Looking Glass*, Chapter Five.

THE AUTHOR

Dr. John Marks OBE is the Director of the Educational Research Trust and was formerly Administrator of the National Council for Educational Standards (NCES). He has been an elected parent/ foundation governor of a comprehensive school since 1978 and has 40 years teaching experience in universities, polytechnics and schools. He sat on the Schools Examination and Assessment Council, 1990-3; the National Curriculum Council, 1992-3; and the Schools Curriculum & Assessment Authority 1993-1997. His publications include *Standards in English Schools* (NCES, 1983 & 1985); *Examination Performance in Secondary Schools in ILEA* (NCES, 1986); *Standards in Schools* (SMF, 1991); *Standards of English & Maths in Primary Schools for 1995*, (SMF, 1996); *Standards of Arithmetic*, (CPS, 1996); *Standards of Reading, Spelling & Maths for 7-year olds in Primary Schools for 1995*, (SMF, 1997*); A Selective or Comprehensive System: which works best?* (CPS, 1998); *An Anatomy of Failure: Standards in English Schools for 1997* (SMF, 1998); *Value for Money in LEA Schools*, (CPS, 1998).

Support towards research for this paper was given by the Institute for Policy Research

© Centre for Policy Studies, June 2000

ISBN No: 1 903219 12 4

Centre for Policy Studies
57 Tufton Street, London SW1P 3QL
Tel: 020 7222 4488 Fax: 020 7222 4388
e-mail: mail@cps.org.uk
website: www.cps.org.uk

Printed by The Chameleon Press, 5 – 25 Burr Road, London SW18

CONTENTS

PPE

SUMMARY

WHAT WE DO KNOW ABOUT SPECIAL EDUCATIONAL NEEDS

1. The numbers of pupils with *Statements of Special Educational Need* has risen from 0.8% to 1.6% in primary schools and from 1.0% to 2.5% in secondary schools over only eight years (from 1991 to 1999).

2. This growth has been accompanied by a deliberate move away from special schools which now accommodate less than 40% of those with Statements – a figure which has fallen from nearer 50% in 1993.

fewer – they are people!

3. The number of pupils with *Special Educational Needs but without Statements* has also risen very rapidly – from 11.6% to 19.2% of pupils in primary schools and from 9.6% to 16.5% in secondary schools over only 4 years from 1995 to 1999.

How do they know?

Expenditure on pupils with Special Educational Needs is impossible to calculate with any accuracy. However, it may be as high as £7.1 billion out of the total education budget of about £20 billion.

4. The total expenditure by schools and LEAs on pupils with Special Educational Needs is impossible to calculate with any accuracy. However, it may be as high as £7.1 billion out of the total education budget of about £20 billion.

i

WHAT WE DON'T KNOW ABOUT SPECIAL EDUCATIONAL NEEDS

1. We don't know – and nobody knows – how much the current Special Educational Needs provision costs or where the money goes or what it is spent on.

2. We don't know – and nobody knows – what the criteria are for pupils with Statements of Special Educational Needs.

3. We don't know – and nobody knows – what the criteria are for pupils with Special Educational Needs at each of Stages One to Four of the Code of Practice.

> *No one knows the criteria for deciding which children have Special Education Needs; nor who they are; nor whether they can read or not; nor whether the current practice is effective or not.*

4. We don't know – and nobody knows – how many pupils with Special Educational Needs there are at each of Stages One to Four of the Code of Practice.

5. We don't know – and nobody knows – how many boys and how many girls have Special Educational Needs of any kind.

6. We don't know – and nobody knows – what types of specific handicap or special need are defined as constituting special needs or how many pupils there are with each specific type of handicap.

7. We don't know – and nobody knows – how many pupils with Special Educational Needs can't read or whether they are being effectively taught to read.

8. We don't know – and nobody knows – whether or not the special arrangements and funding for pupils with Special Educational Needs improves pupils' learning or increases their knowledge.

WHAT ARE THE CAUSES OF THE RISE IN SPECIAL EDUCATIONAL NEEDS

Nobody can be sure of the causes behind this increase in the numbers of children being assessed as having Special Education Needs but the likeliest candidates are the changes in primary practice following the publication and implementation of the Plowden Report (1967). The emergence of the "disorderly classroom" and the related retreat from traditional teaching methods (in particular, phonics) are likely to have been a major factor.

HOW TO REDUCE THE NUMBER OF PUPILS WITH SPECIAL EDUCATION NEEDS

1. Withdraw the Code of Practice

The Code of Practice should be withdrawn because it is so imprecise as to be virtually meaningless and hence, as ample experience and evidence have shown, is unenforceable in practice.

2. Annual monitoring of reading

All special needs pupils should be required to take externally administered standardised tests of reading and spelling each year which should determine whether or not the particular policies – and associated funding – should continue.

3. Reforming teaching practices and school organisation

The inefficiency and disruption caused in many schools by much current special needs provision could be considerably reduced:

- by abandoning the policy of 'inclusion', especially if this involves reducing the number of mixed-ability classes;

- by teaching reading earlier and more effectively;

- by increasing academic selection both within and between schools;

- by introducing the continental practice of repeating a year.

WHAT MUST BE DONE TO HELP THOSE WITH REAL SPECIAL EDUCATIONAL NEEDS

1. Special Schools

The case for special schools is much stronger now than it was in the early 1980s especially since the development of the National Curriculum. Many parents actually prefer special schools to mainstream schools and many teachers favour inclusion more in theory than in practice.

2. Reform or Abolish Statements?

The concept of the individual pupil's Statement of Special Educational Need in its present form may have outlived its usefulness.

3. Reassess categories of disability

The concept of defining specific categories of disability should be revived.

4. A National Enquiry

A National Enquiry should be set up to establish the scale of the present use (and misuse) of resources, to monitor the effects of the changes proposed to reduce the number of pupils classified as having Special Educational Needs and to review the provision for pupils with real Special Educational Needs.

Existing policies on Special Educational Needs must be rigorously tested – in the interests of all those pupils who have over the years been failed by 'the system'.

CHAPTER ONE
INTRODUCTION

Since the 1970s, there has been a substantial growth in arrangements set up to look after pupils identified as having Special Educational Needs (or "SEN"). This has been accompanied by a rising tide of superficially persuasive rhetoric – emanating from a large special needs lobby and speaking a language which is often ambiguous but which gives the appearance of being compassionate.[1]

There are two classes of children with Special Education Needs: those with serious physical and/or mental disabilities (about 2% to 3% of children); and another 20% who are at any one time are judged to have "learning difficulties".

There are two classes of Special Education Needs:

- those classified as having explicit "Statements of Special Education Need" – between 2 to 3% of all pupils. Typically, these children will have serious physical and/or mental disabilities which hinder their learning ability;

- those classified as having "Special Educational Needs but without Statements". Nearly 20% of children in England are now classified as such.

---

[1] This is apparent in parliamentary debates on Special Educational Needs in both Houses of Parliament and in the workings of educational bodies like the School Examinations and Assessment Council (SEAC), the National Curriculum Council (NCC) & the Schools Curriculum and Assessment Authority (SCAA) on which I served for 7 years.

The numbers of children in both categories have grown rapidly in recent years, especially in England.

It is important to distinguish those with real special needs – the 2 to 3% with Statements – from those who may be classified as having special needs – the 20% or so without Statements. This paper will put forward the hypothesis that the main problem with the 20% may be that they have not been properly taught, (and in particular not been properly taught how to read) in their early years at school.

Once the 20% can be distinguished from the 2 to 3%, a more focused and much needed debate can take place about the best way to educate those with real and serious Special Educational Needs.

Many people may recoil from a fundamental review of such a sensitive area of educational policy. But, given the present lack of clarity about what is happening and where all the money is going, it is surely time to ask some fundamental questions in the interests of all the pupils involved. In particular, should all these children be included in main-stream schools or should existing special schools be retained and developed? And how can scarce educational resources be best used to help those most in need?.

CHAPTER TWO
ORIGINS AND GROWTH

The origins of the explosion in Special Educational Needs lie in the report of the Warnock Committee[2] in 1978 and the resulting 1981 Education Act. This Act, passed with all-party support, set up the system of Statements of Special Educational Need.

This replaced a system in which ten categories of disability were statutorily defined. The number of pupils involved was around 2% of the cohort. They were mainly educated in special schools.

The Warnock Committee made two main changes. First, it introduced the terminology of 'special need' which focuses on the educational provision the pupil requires rather than identifying what is 'wrong' with them.[3] Secondly it extended the concept of special need so that it included:

> ...perhaps, up to 20% of the school population.[4]

Those concerned with education welcomed this extension and research in the early 1980s as it showed that it corresponded with what class teachers saw as the scale of special needs.[5]

---

2   *Committee of Enquiry into the Education of Handicapped Children and Young People* (chaired by Mary Warnock), Department of Education & Science, 1978.

3   By deciding into which, if any, of the 10 statutory categories does the individual pupil fall.

4   P Croll and D Moses, *Special Need in the Primary School: One in Five?*, Cassell, 2000, p 2.

5   P Croll and D Moses, *One in Five*, Routledge & Kegan Paul, 1985.

The rapid growth in the numbers officially classified as having Special Educational Needs came later after the introduction of the *Code of Practice on the Identification and Assessment of Special Educational Needs* (1994; currently being revised) – a bulky document but not as bulky as the procedures and structures to which it has led.

The *Code* has over 400 paragraphs, comes with three sets of Statutory Regulations[6] and six Circulars[7] and lays down five Stages of Special Educational Need. Stages One to Three are applied solely within schools[8] while Stages Four and Five – movement towards, and possession of, Statements – involve both schools and LEAs.

The Code of Practice *does not contain any precise criteria for defining the various Stages of SEN. Nor does it define specific types of disability. Its own definition is remarkably circular.*

It is most striking that neither the *Code* nor its supporting documents contains any precise criteria for defining the various Stages – a fact which is recognised professionally.[9] Nor does the *Code* identify and define specific types of disability by name. Instead it gives this marvellously circular and open-ended definition:

> A child has *Special Educational Needs* if he or she has a *learning difficulty* which calls for *special educational provision* to be made for him or her.[10]

As a Working Party of The British Psychological Society puts it:

---

6   The following Regulations are relevant to the Code: the *Education (Special Educational Needs) Regulations 1994*, which are attached to the Code; the *Education (Special Educational Needs) (Information) Regulations 1994*, which are summarised in the Code and attached to and enlarge upon the Circular on the *Organisation of Special Educational Provision*, which is published alongside the Code; the *Education (Payment for Special Educational Needs Supplies) Regulations 1994* which are also covered in the Circular on the *Organisation of Special Educational Provision*.

7   A package of six Circulars on 'Pupils with Problems': *Pupil behaviour and discipline; The education of children with emotional and behavioural difficulties; Exclusions from school; The education by LEAs of children otherwise than at school; The education of sick children;* and *The education of children being looked after by local authorities.*

8   According to the *Code*, Stage 1 in the Code's model is characterised by the gathering of information and increased differentiation within the child's normal classroom work while Stages 2 and 3 are characterised, respectively, by the creation of individual education plans and the involvement of outside specialists.

9   See *Section 6.1 The Concept of Special Educational Needs* in *Dyslexia, Literacy and Psychological Assessment*, The British Psychological Society, 1999, pp 56-7.

10   The *Code*, paragraph 2.1.

In reality, the learning difficulty and the special educational needs are one and the same thing. Special educational needs are a *post hoc*, child-centred construction of the learning difficulty following from the agreement to respond to the learning difficulty with provision that is considered to be special.[11]

Nevertheless, despite this imprecision and circularity of definition, the *Code* confidently states that:

Nationally, about 20% of children may have some form of Special Educational Needs at some time.[12]

This is one of the few educational targets which has now been reached and which is in danger of being over-fulfilled.

11   Reference 9, p 57.
12   The *Code*, paragraph 2.2.

CHAPTER THREE
NUMBERS OF SEN PUPILS WITH STATEMENTS

It is important to consider separately *pupils with Statements* and *pupils with Special Educational Needs but without Statements*. The two groups are very different and the numbers involved are virtually uncorrelated for both schools and LEAs. This Chapter looks at the data for those children with statements (i.e. those children with the greatest difficulties); Chapter Four looks at those without Statements.

There is a further sub-division with those pupils who are classified as having Special Education Needs with Statements: some attend mainstream schools; others go to special schools and to Pupil Referral Units.

> *In England, the proportion of children with Statements has risen from 0.8% to 1.6% in primary schools and from 1.0% to 2.5% in secondary schools in just eight years.*

PUPILS WITH STATEMENTS IN MAINSTREAM SCHOOLS

In England, the proportion of pupils with Statements has risen rapidly from 0.8% to 1.6% in primary schools and from 1.0% to 2.5% in secondary schools over only eight years (1991-1999). There are now more than 10,000 pupils in each age cohort and a total of nearly 150,000 pupils with Statements in mainstream schools. (See Table 1 & Figure 1)

TABLE I. PUPILS WITH STATEMENTS OF SEN, ENGLAND, 1991-99

Year	Number in Primary Schools	% in Primary Schools	Number in Secondary Schools	% in Secondary Schools	Number in All Schools	% in All Schools
1991	32,655	0.8	29,058	1.0	61,713	0.9
1992	36,379	0.9	34,562	1.2	70,941	1.0
1993	43,464	1.0	41,114	1.4	84,578	1.2
1994	50,112	1.2	50,142	1.7	100,254	1.4
1995	55,768	1.3	57,040	1.9	112,808	1.5
1996	61,698	1.4	65,137	2.2	126,835	1.7
1997	63,551	1.4	70,080	2.3	133,631	1.8
1998	67,014	1.5	73,951	2.4	140,965	1.9
1999	69,833	1.6	77,370	2.5	147,203	2.0

FIGURE I

Percentage of Pupils with Statements of SEN,
England 1991-99

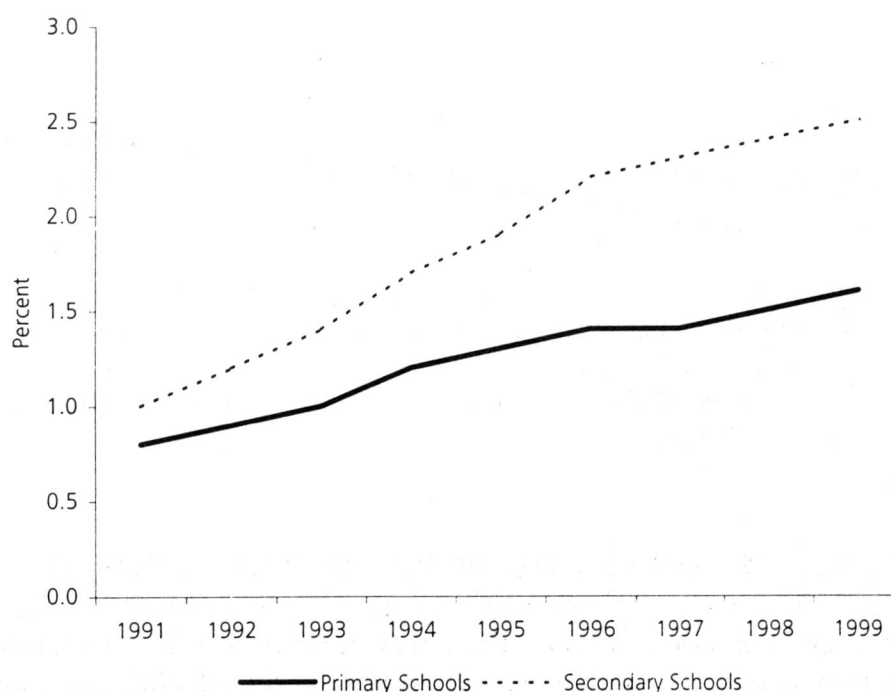

—— Primary Schools · · · · · Secondary Schools

In Wales the proportion of pupils with Statements is higher than in England –
3.4% rising from about 2.5% in the mid 1980s.

For primary school pupils in Scotland the proportion of pupils with Statements
is much lower than in either England or Wales – 0.9% rising from about 0.1%
in the mid 1980s and 0.4% in 1991; no data are available for secondary pupils in
Scotland.

In Northern Ireland the percentage of pupils with Statements is also lower –
1.3%, rising from 0.4% in 1989 and 1% in 1995.

FIGURE 2

Percentage of pupils with Statements in Mainstream Schools in Wales &
Scotland, 1984-98

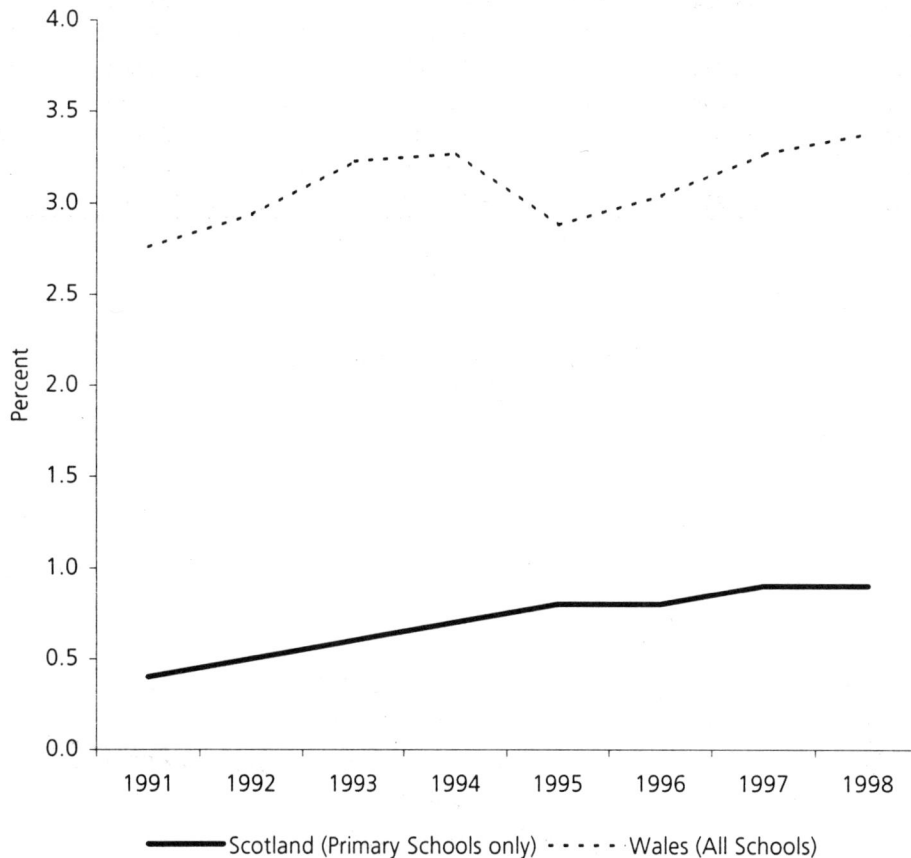

SPECIAL SCHOOLS AND PUPIL REFERRAL UNITS

The growth in pupils with Statements has been accompanied by a deliberate
move away from special schools. These now accommodate less than 40% of
those with Statements,[13] rather than almost 50% in 1993.[14] While the number
of children with Statements in mainstream schools increased from about 60,000
to 150,000 over eight years, the number in special schools has remained
virtually static at about 80,000.

---

13   *Special Education 1994-98: A Review of Special Schools, Secure Units and Pupil Referral Units
      in England*, Ofsted, 1999.

14   *Special Educational Needs in England: January 1998*, Statistical Bulletin 9/98. DfEE,
      October 1998; *Special Educational Needs in England: January 1999*, Statistical Bulletin
      12/99. DfEE, October 1999.

Numbers of pupils with Statements in Mainstream Schools and Special
Schools in England, 1991-99

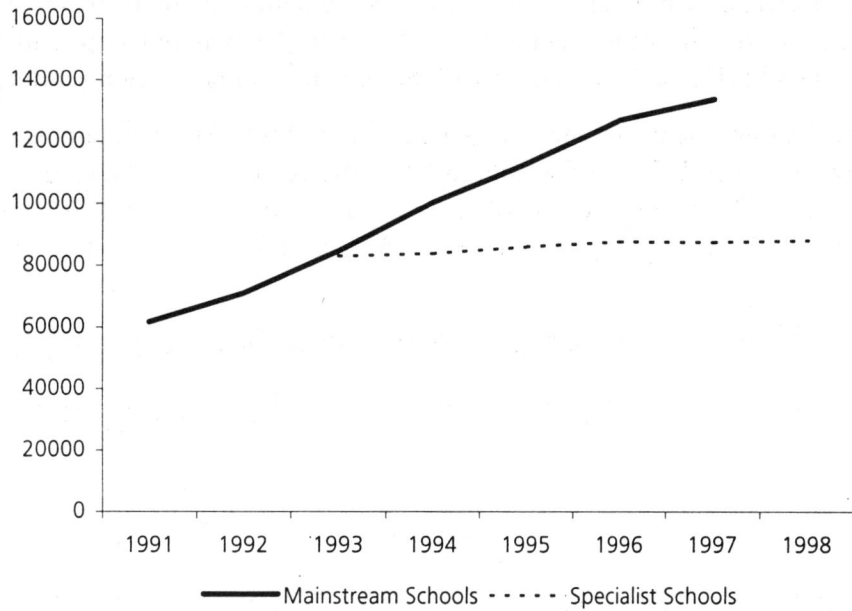

FIGURE 3

DATA FOR LOCAL EDUCATION AUTHORITIES (LEAs)

Figure 4 shows the mean percentage of pupils on School Rolls with Statements
in LEAs in England in 1998; the vertical scale shows the number of LEAs. The
average for all LEAs is 2.6% but the range is wide: from as few as 0.5% of
pupils with Statements in mainstream schools; to over 5%.

FIGURE 4

Distribution of Children with Statements on School Rolls, LEAs in England,
1998

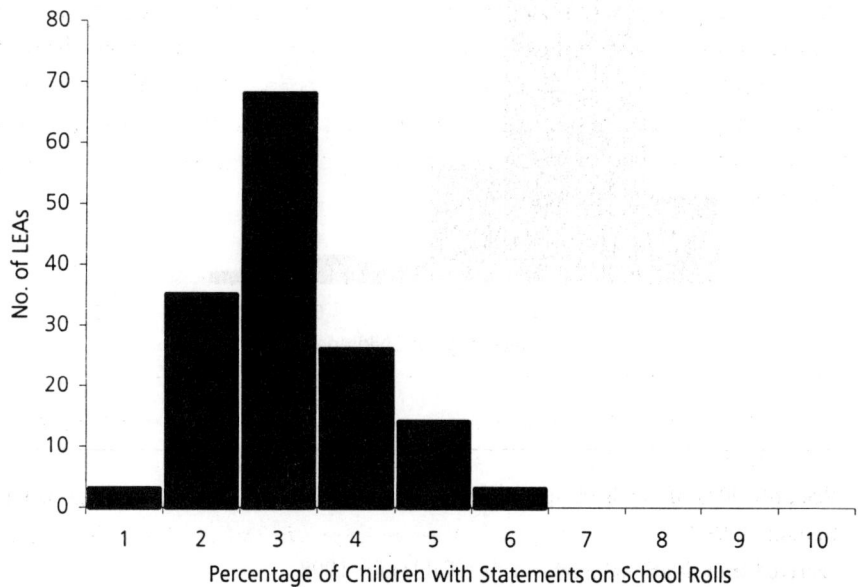

9

Practice differs widely between LEAs. Some LEAs have many more pupils with Statements in Special Schools or Pupil Referral Units and fewer with Statements in ordinary schools while in other LEAs the reverse is the case.[15] For example Reading has 5.7% of its 15-year-old pupils in Special Schools and Pupil Referral Units and 1.4% with Statements in mainstream schools. Shropshire, on the other hand, has 1.1% of its 15-year-old pupils in Special Schools and 5.1% of 15-year-olds with Statements in mainstream schools.

Figure 5 shows the mean percentage of 15-year-olds in Special Schools or Pupil Referral Units in LEAs in England in 1998; the vertical scale shows the number of LEAs.[16] The average for all LEAs is 2.2% but again the range is wide: from as few as 0.4% of pupils with Statements in Special Schools to up to 6.5%.

Some LEAs and some schools have very few pupils with Statements; others have a much higher proportion.

FIGURE 5

Proportion of 15 year old pupils with Statements on School Rolls or Pupil Referral Units, LEAs in England, 1998

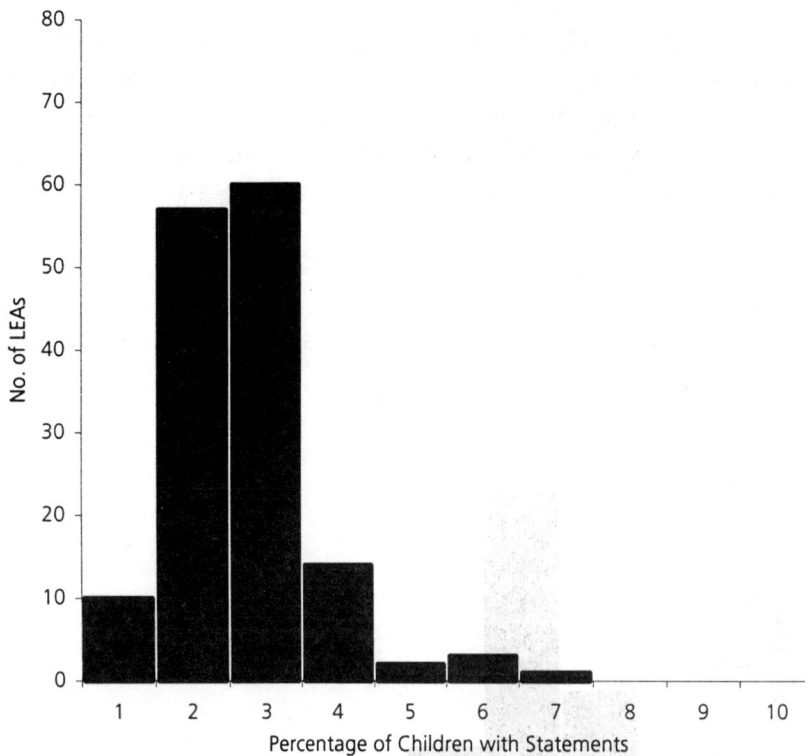

---

15   Roughly 90% of pupils in Special Schools and 25% of pupils in Pupil Referral Units have Statements.

16   Derived from National Performance Tables for 1998.

DATA FOR INDIVIDUAL SCHOOLS

Individual schools vary widely in the proportion of their pupils who are classified as having Special Education Needs with Statements. Some have less than 1%; others have more than 14% (see Figure 6 – the vertical scale shows the number of schools). Similar data for primary schools are not available but the variations are likely to be of a similar magnitude or possibly even greater.

FIGURE 6

Proportion of pupils with Statements on School Rolls, Secondary Schools in England, 1998

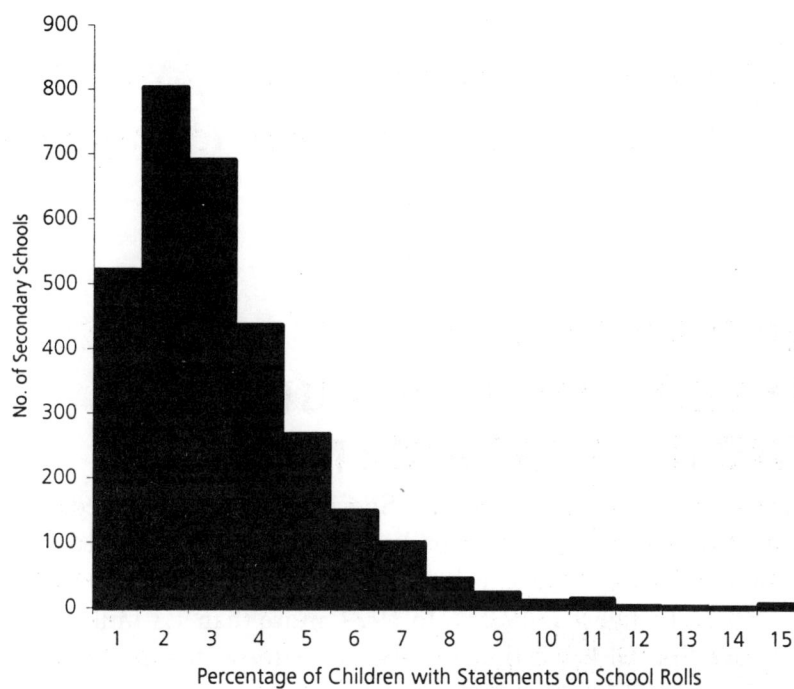

CHAPTER FOUR
NUMBERS OF SEN PUPILS
WITHOUT STATEMENTS

In England, the number of pupils with Special Educational Needs but without Statements is now very large. In secondary schools, on average, 16.5% of pupils are classified as having Special Educational Needs at Stages One to Four; in primary schools the figure is 19.2%. In 1999, more than 1.3 million pupils were judged to have Special Education Needs (but without Statements) – and more than 140,000 pupils in each age cohort in primary schools.[17]

In 1999, more than 1.3 million children were diagnosed as having Special Education Needs but without Statements. In 1995, the same figure was under 800,000.

The proportion of children with SEN but without Statements has risen very rapidly – from 11.6% to 19.2% in primary schools and from 9.6% to 16.5% in secondary schools over only four years from 1995 to 1999. (see Table 2 and Figure 7).

---

[17] No data are available for pupils in Scotland, Wales and Northern Ireland with Special Educational Needs but without Statements.

TABLE II. PUPILS WITH SEN BUT WITHOUT STATEMENTS ENGLAND, 1991-99

Year	Number in Primary Schools	% in Primary Schools	Number in Secondary Schools	% in Secondary Schools	Number in All Schools
1995	500,209	11.6	287,753	9.6	787,962
1996	691,414	15.8	392,996	13.1	1,084,410
1997	759,449	17.1	442,024	14.5	1,201,473
1998	821,342	18.4	479,675	15.6	1,301,017
1999	859,850	19.2	514,483	16.5	1,374,333

FIGURE 7

Percentage of Pupils with SEN but without a Statement

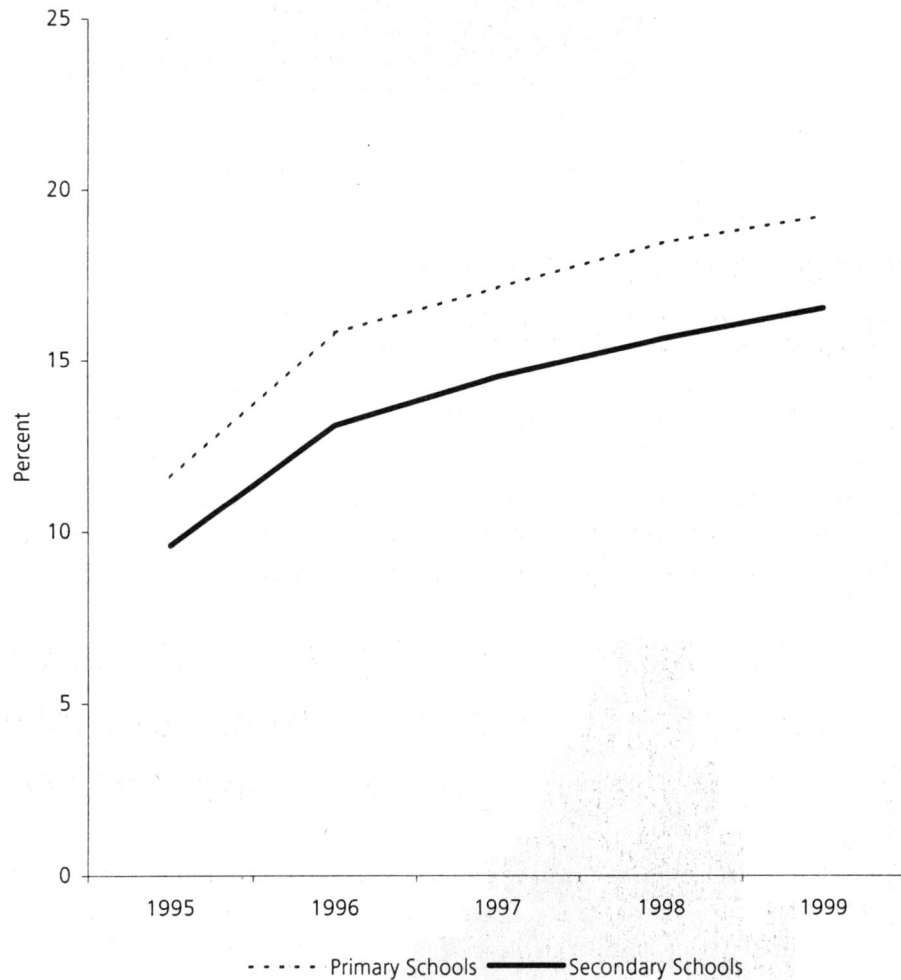

- - - - - Primary Schools ———Secondary Schools

DATA FOR LOCAL EDUCATION AUTHORITIES (LEAS)

Figure 8 shows the mean percentage of pupils on School Rolls with Statements in LEAs in England in 1998; the vertical scale shows the number of LEAs. The average for all LEAs is 16.9% but the range is wide – from 7.8% to the very high figure of 32.6%.

FIGURE 8

Proportion of pupils with Special Education Needs but without Statements on School Rolls, LEAs in England, 1998

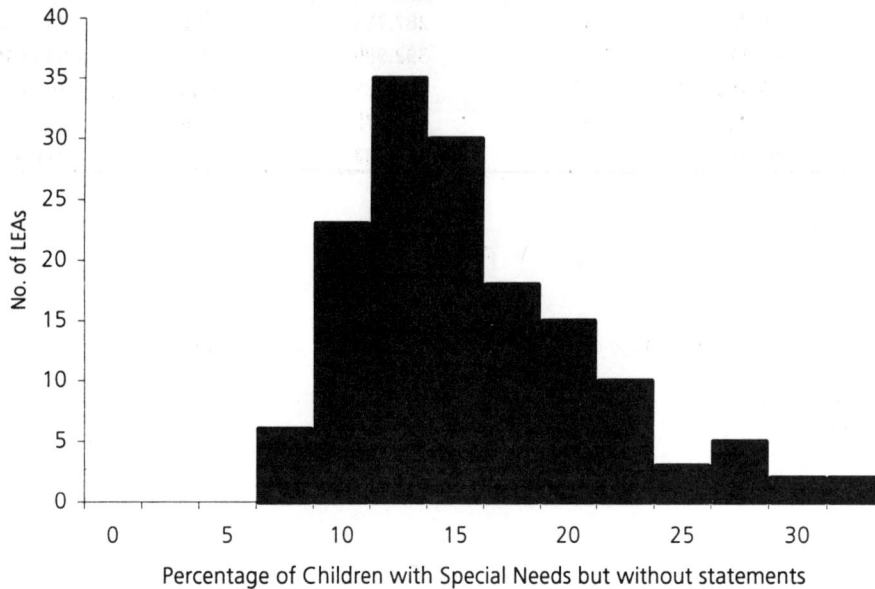

DATA FOR INDIVIDUAL SCHOOLS

Individual schools vary widely in the percentages of pupils on roll with Special Educational Needs but without Statements.

FIGURE 9

Proportion of pupils with Special Education Needs but without Statements on School Rolls, Secondary Schools in England, 1998

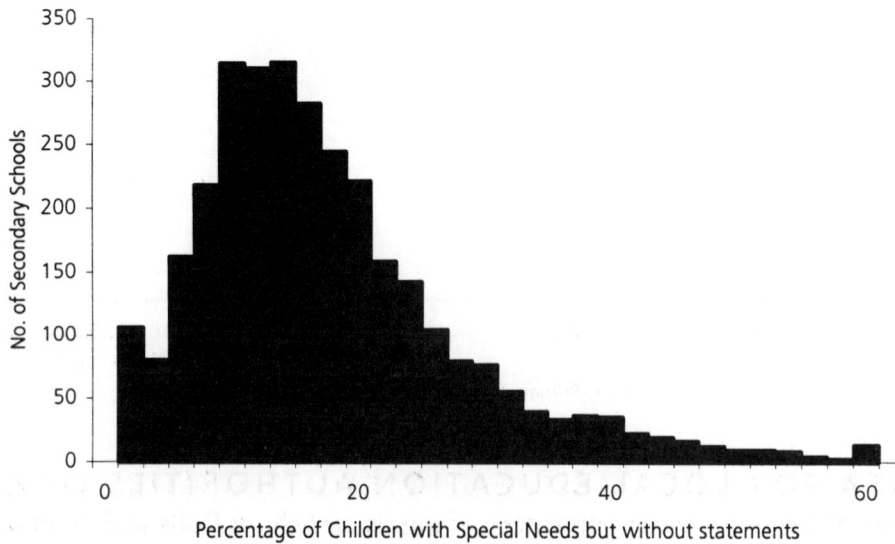

Data for secondary schools from performance tables show that the percentages of pupils on roll with Special Educational Needs but without Statements averages 16.5% but varies very widely – from less than 1% to a staggering 55% or more in some schools; the maximum is 79.5%.

Data for primary schools is not available but the variations are likely to be of a similar magnitude.

In one school, 79.5% of children are diagnosed as having Special Education Needs.

CONCLUSION

The extraordinary growth in the number of pupils with Special Educational Needs but without Statements – towards the 'target' set by the Warnock Committee and the *Code of Practice* – needs further study.

But before discussing this topic it is important to assess the costs of the current provision of Special Educational Needs – a question which has no satisfactory answer.

CHAPTER FIVE
WHAT DOES IT COST?

All this costs a great deal of money in LEAs and in schools but exactly how much is not clear. In the early 1990s, some LEAs spent about 12% of their budgets on Special Educational Needs. With a doubling in the number of children classified as having Special Educational Needs, it is likely to be even more now. According to a recent article in *The Economist*, which made use of DfEE figures:

> The budget for special-needs education is £2.5 billion a year and rising...[18]

Indeed *The Economist* suggests that the current revision of the *Code of Practice* may, in part, be due to fear of rising costs which could undermine the Government's other educational programmes.

Is the Government worried that the rising cost of helping SEN pupils takes funds from other education initiatives?

In the United States,[19] which has many parallels with this country, there are widespread fears that the costs of special education are rising too fast and are increasingly threatening the funding of mainstream education.[20] The same may well be true here.

---

[18]   "Making a statement", *The Economist*, 8 January, 2000, p 33.

[19]   See M McLaughlin & M Rouse (ed.), *Special Education & School Reform in the United States & Britain*, , Routledge, 2000 for further discussion.

[20]   T Parrish, *Special Education Finance*, Federal Resource Centre for Special Education, Washington DC, 1997.

PERVERSE INCENTIVES

The system of SEN contains two perverse incentives. First, the system has a vested interest in failure: the more children with Special Educational Needs that can be identified, the greater are the resources that can be claimed.

The system has a vested interest in failure: the more children with SEN that can be identified, the greater the resources that can be claimed.

Secondly, the rapid rise from the mid-1990s in the numbers of pupils with Special Educational Needs but without Statements coincided with the publication of National Performance Tables – from 1992 for secondary schools giving results for GCSE and A-level and from 1995 for primary schools giving the National Curriculum test results for 11 year olds.

Could it be that some schools are finding it helpful to try to explain their relatively poor showing in these tables by pointing to their high percentages of pupils with Special Educational Needs but without Statements?[21]

HOW LEAs SPEND MONEY ON SEN

LEAs are responsible for procedures for issuing Statements and for providing money to schools – via school funding formulae – for pupils in schools with Statements and more generally for pupils at Stages 1-4 of the *Code* .

The only available published data show expenditure by LEAs on pupils with Statements rose from £290 million in 1995 to £370 million in 1999 with about a further £90 million each year on other pupils with Special Educational Needs.[22] These figures do not represent the full total of LEA expenditure.

In addition to the costs of issuing and supporting Statements, LEAs face substantial expenditure if parents appeal to the statutory Special Educational Needs Tribunal whose decisions are legally binding on the LEA.[23]

HOW SCHOOLS SPEND MONEY ON SEN

In addition to the money spent by LEAs, a substantial sum is spent by schools on providing SEN education. Schools spend money on Special Educational Needs in three main ways:

---

[21]   It is true that the implementation of the *Code* after 1994 may have been a contributing factor but nevertheless the parallels are striking, particularly since no similar rise appears to have taken place in either Wales or Scotland where Performance Tables either do not exist or are less well-publicised than in England.

[22]   Data from LEA financial statements under Section 42/122 of the 1988/1996 Education Acts listed as a discretionary exception for Special Educational Needs.

[23]   Tribunal rulings have led to some LEAs funding children at boarding schools overseas, such as the Higashi School in Boston which specialises in educating autistic children.

- on reducing class sizes in lower sets;

- on providing classroom assistants to help special needs pupils in class – frequently by writing assignments in pupils workbooks;

- on administration by Special Educational Needs Co-ordinators (SENCOs) who revise Statements annually for pupils with Statements and write, and revise termly, Individual Education Plans (IEPs) for Stages 2-4 special needs. IEPs consume much staff time and paper, are often too complex to be used effectively by teachers and are seldom consulted except by Ofsted during inspections.[24]

The complexities can perhaps best be illustrated by an example. Table 3 shows the Special Educational Needs expenditure for one London LEA for one year.[25]

TABLE III. ANNUAL SPECIAL EDUCATIONAL NEEDS BUDGET IN ONE LEA

Category	Total %	Total £ million
Retained by LEA for SEN education	12.9%	£17.5 million
Delegated directly to schools for SEN education	3.7%	£5.0 million
Delegated implicitly to schools for SEN education[26]	2.6%	£3.5 million
Total Special Educational Needs Budget	**19.2%**	**£26.0 million**
Total Education Budget	100%	£135.5 million

The amount retained by the LEA includes the costs of:

- pupils at special schools and pupils referral units;

- support for pupils with Statements and for specialist units in mainstream schools;

- educational psychologists and other specialist staff;

- transport for pupils with Special Educational Needs.

Expenditure on children with SEN is estimated to be £7.1 billion, out of an education budget of £20 billion.

If the same percentage – 19.2% – of the education budget were spent nationally the expenditure on Special Educational Needs pupils would be about £3.8 billion out of the total education budget of about £20 billion – a figure which is even higher than that quoted by *The Economist*.

---

24   See *The SEN Code of Practice: three years on – the contribution of individual education plans to the raising of standards for pupils with special educational needs*, Ofsted, 1999 for more information on IEPs; the report states that:

> The placement on the SEN register is the trigger – not whether an IEP is thought to be useful or will be particularly relevant in any individual case. (p 6)

25   This section is based on Table 8.1 and the related discussion in M McLaughlin & M Rouse (ed.), *Special Education & School Reform in the United States & Britain*, Routledge, 2000, pp 173 et seq.

26   See *the SEN Initiative: Managing budgets for Pupils with Special Educational Needs*, Coopers & Lybrand, 1996 which estimates that the 'non-specific' special needs element may range from 5.3 % to 16% of the per pupil funding unit; the lower of these two figures is used here.

If the money also spent on these pupils from the rest of the schools budget is included, the total expenditure on Special Educational Needs pupils is estimated to be about £7.1 billion.[27]

A recent survey of 85 LEAs showed that the main factors used to make budgetary allocations via funding formulae to schools for pupils with Special Educational Needs but without Statements were cheap but unspecific indicators (such as average take-up of free school meals and, more rarely, average levels of attainment in schools). Relatively expensive and time consuming procedures to audit individual pupil needs were also used but in a minority of cases.[28]

LACK OF ACCOUNTABILITY

There is a grave lack of accountability for funds intended to be used for SEN pupils. In particular, both the money provided for pupils with Statements in mainstream schools and the formula-funded money do not have to be spent on the specific pupils involved; nor even specifically on special needs.

There is a grave lack of accountability throughout the system: money provided for a pupil with SEN does not have to be spent on that pupil, or even on SEN provision.

According to one recent paper:[29]

> For 'non-Statemented' Special Educational Needs.....particularly at Stage 3, schools get extra money and are expected to provide smaller groups or extra help when a child is placed at this stage. Yet the LEA has no power to see that the help is provided.

Moreover:

> Under the current UK system of financial delegation, funding for non-statemented SEN can easily be cut by the LEA, never reaching the school. If it does get there, the school's management can choose to use it for other purposes.

For this reason, some LEAs are now trying to delegate funding – with the intention of ring-fencing the money for Special Educational Needs – rather than to devolve funding – which gives schools the power to decide whether or not to use the money for SEN or some other purpose.[30]

---

27   20% – the percentage of SEN pupils – of the 80.8% left after the specific SEN funding is excluded – is 16.2% giving a grand total of (19.2 + 16.2)% or 35.4% of about £20 billion or £7.1 billion.

28   A Marsh, *Current Practice for Resourcing Additional Needs in Local Education Authorities*, NFER, 1997; see F Fletcher-Campbell *The Resourcing of Special Educational Needs*, NFER, 1996 for more information on audits in particular.

29   M McLaughlin & M Rouse (ed.), *Special Education & School Reform in the United States & Britain*, , Routledge, 2000, pp 173-4.

30   *The SEN Initiative: Managing budgets for pupils with special educational needs*, Coopers & Lybrand, Phase 1, 1996; Phase 2, 1998.

Nor are the funding or the policies or the structures accountable in the sense that improvements in pupil performance have to be shown to result from the chosen special needs policies or from the specific extra funding provided. As has been pointed out:

> A good example of the failure to evaluate the effectiveness of outcomes can be found in fact that the equivalent of 24,000 full-time unqualified assistants are currently used to support SEN in mainstream schools.[31] A cautious estimate of the cost of their direct employment would suggest that this is the equivalent to the entire education budgets of more than two London LEAs or, put another way, enough to fund more than five hundred primary (elementary) schools. Yet little has been done to determine how effective this resource is in achieving educational goals.[32]

The scale of the staffing involved can also be appreciated by scanning the job vacancies in the *Times Educational Supplement*. In a typical issue there 24 pages of advertisements for SEN-related posts including, for example, at a salary of up to more than £56,000, the Principal of a new "EBD School and Support Service" established in response to a Special School Review Programme.

> This new development will encompass a day special school (EBD), outreach work, multi-agency support and EBD Support Services to mainstream schools within an integrated single management structure.

The LEA involved has recently been severely criticised by Ofsted both in general and for its inadequate Special Needs services.

Nor do improvements in pupil performance have to be shown to result from either any specific special needs policy or from the specific extra funding provided.

CONCLUSION

We don't know, and nobody knows:

- how much the current Special Educational Needs provision costs; or,

- where the money goes; or,

- whether or not it is spent on SEN provision; or,

- whether or not it has any effect on the educational attainment of the pupils concerned.

---

31 *Excellence for all Children*, DfEE, 1997.

32 M McLaughlin & M Rouse (ed.), *Special Education & School Reform in the United States & Britain*, , Routledge, 2000, p. 179.

CHAPTER SIX
SIX QUESTIONS NO ONE CAN ANSWER
WHAT ARE THE CRITERIA FOR DECIDING WHETHER A CHILD HAS SPECIAL EDUCATIONAL NEEDS?

Criteria for Statements

In 1992 the Audit Commission[33] suggested national criteria for deciding which children should have a Statement but so far, no definitive criteria exist or have been proposed.[34]

Criteria for Stages One to Four

No criteria exist for distinguishing between pupils at each of the Stages One to Four of the *Code of Practice.* except for the very crude procedural definitions outlined in the *Code* itself and quoted above. The result is that the criteria used in practice are likely to vary considerably from school to school.

HOW MANY PUPILS ARE AT THE VARIOUS STAGES OF SEN?

No data are available about the numbers of pupils at each of the Stages from One to Four of the *Code of Practice.*

WHO ARE THE CHILDREN WITH SEN?

The only extensive data on the numbers of pupils with different types of Special Educational Needs are those for Wales. These are derived mainly from the annual census of schools.[35]

---

33   *Getting in on the Act*, Audit Commission, 1992.

34   M McLaughlin & M Rouse (ed.), *Special Education & School Reform in the United States & Britain*, Routledge, 2000, p 171.

In 1998, about 50% of pupils with Statements in all schools were classified as having either Moderate or Severe Learning Difficulties; about a further 10% had Emotional and Behavioural Difficulties. Pupils with Specific Learning Difficulties (Dyslexia) made up about 18% of pupils with Statements in all schools (they were overwhelmingly in mainstream schools). Those with a range of Physical Disabilities – including Autism, Hearing and/or Visual Impairment, and Speech and Communication Difficulties – made up about 18% of pupils with Statements in all schools and about 15% in special schools.

Data from Ofsted for special schools in England in 1998 show a similar pattern. Over 70% had either Moderate or Severe Learning Difficulties and a further 10% had Emotional & Behavioural Difficulties. Another 10% had the range of Physical Disabilities mentioned above. Ofsted have also published a survey of provision in mainstream schools for pupils with Statements relating to Specific Learning Difficulties (Dyslexia)[36] but this does not give data for the whole country.

HOW MANY BOYS AND GIRLS HAVE SEN?
Numbers and Percentages of Boys and Girls with Statements
Very little or no information is available about the numbers and percentages of boys and girls with Statements. However, data from Ofsted for 1998 show that there were twice as many boys as girls in special schools in England – about 67,000 (67%) compared with about 33,000 (33%).

No other data are available for England for pupils with Statements either in primary or secondary schools.

More data are available for Wales (again, mainly from the annual census of schools). In 1998 there were 11,800 boys (70%) with Statements in all schools compared with 4,900 girls (30%).[37] Similar proportions of boys and girls with Statements are in mainstream schools in Wales – in 1998 there were 4,400 boys (70.4%) and 1,800 girls (29.6%) in primary schools and 4,800 boys (72%) and 1,900 girls (28%) in secondary schools.[38]

Boys outnumber girls in all the specific categories mentioned above but in proportions varying from 55% to 85%.

No data are available for Scotland or Northern Ireland.

Numbers and Percentages of Boys & Girls with Special Educational Needs but without Statements.
No data of any kind are available for any of the countries of the United Kingdom.

---

35   *Special Education Provision in Wales*, Statistical Brief SDB 7/99, Welsh Office Statistical Directorate, January 1999, Tables 10-12.

36   *Pupils with specific learning difficulties in mainstream schools*, Ofsted, 1999.

37   *Special Education Provision in Wales*, Statistical Brief SDB 7/99, Welsh Office Statistical Directorate, January 1999, Table 12.

38   *Wales: SEN Pupil Numbers*, House of Lords Hansard, Col WA 139, 11 May, 1999.

CAN SEN PUPILS READ?

It is estimated that the main problem with about 75% of special needs pupils, both now and a decade ago, is that they can't read.[39]

Yet little special needs money is used to monitor this, or to teach these pupils to read. Few special needs pupils are withdrawn from ordinary classrooms for the systematic teaching and monitoring of reading for any considerable time, even if this is what they need and often want. The ideology of 'inclusion' and of 'access' to the National Curriculum' is too strong.

In addition there are many pupils who can't read but who are never identified as non-readers or as having Special Educational Needs. In one study of 11-year-olds, over half those identified as being two or more years behind in reading were not identified as having special needs.[40]

DO THE SPECIAL ARRANGEMENTS AND FUNDING IMPROVE PUPILS' LEARNING OR INCREASE THEIR KNOWLEDGE?

No procedures exist to monitor this.

---

39   In Croydon in the late 1980s, 75% of the referrals to the school psychological service were attributable to poor reading (M Turner, private communication); see also M Turner, *Just another education industry* in *The Independent*, 26 September, 1991.

40   T Burkard, *Literacy: identification of special needs in primary school* in *British Journal of Curriculum & Assessment*, Vol 8, No 3, Summer 1998, pp 10-12.

CHAPTER SEVEN
OTHER EFFECTS OF SPECIAL EDUCATIONAL NEEDS

Special needs provision has had a considerable effect on the National Curriculum, on National Curriculum testing and on public examinations.

Throughout the writing of the National Curriculum the principle has been respected that, wherever possible, special needs pupils should have access to the same curriculum as other pupils.

This praiseworthy aspiration has, however, sometimes led to pressures to lower expectations in what the National Curriculum requires, especially at Key Stage 1.

Many special needs pupils do not take National Curriculum tests. For those that do, special arrangements can be made which, especially in primary schools, provide loopholes for early opening of test papers and possible cheating. Ministers have insisted on more rigorous procedures at Key Stages 2 & 3, but not yet at Key Stage 1. Very little information is collected and published about how many pupils are involved, and for what reason, and in what way they are assisted.

The formerly fairly strict procedures for special needs pupils in GCSE examinations have recently been made less rigorous in ways which threaten to undermine national standards. Once again, nobody knows how many pupils and which schools are involved and what are the reasons for special treatment.[41]

---

41 At Winchester last year 37 pupils out of cohort of 144 were allowed "special arrangements" in GCSE examinations – at 26% this is an over-fulfilled norm compared with the National Target of about 20% set two decades ago by Warnock and the profession and restated in the 1994 Code of Practice.

CHAPTER EIGHT
THE NEED FOR RADICAL REFORM

The previous Chapters have shown that:

- We don't know – and nobody knows – what the criteria are for pupils with Statements of Special Educational Needs.

- We don't know – and nobody knows – what the criteria are for pupils with Special Educational Needs at each of Stages One to Four of the *Code of Practice*.

- We don't know – and nobody knows – how many pupils with Special Educational Needs there are at each of Stages One to Four of the *Code of Practice*.

- We don't know – and nobody knows – how many boys and how many girls have Special Educational Needs of any kind.

- We don't know – and nobody knows – what types of specific disability or special need are defined as constituting special needs, or how many pupils there are with each specific type of handicap.

- We don't know – and nobody knows – how many pupils with Special Educational Needs can't read or whether they are being effectively taught to read.

- We don't know – and nobody knows – whether or not the special arrangements and funding for pupils with Special Educational Needs improve pupils' learning or increase their knowledge.

This list of unanswered questions is far too long. Money is going in increasingly large amounts into a Black Hole of unknown and possibly unknowable size.

There is no serious public accountability in the procedures which now deal with more than a fifth of all pupils and over a third of the total education budget. And the present system cannot be made more accountable, given the current lack of precision in the definition of, and criteria for, Special Educational Needs, together with the opacity of the funding arrangements.

> *There is negligible accountability for the procedures which now deal with a fifth of all pupils and a third of the total education budget.*

THE GOVERNMENT'S PROPOSALS

There is thus a clear need for major reforms. However, at this stage, it seems that the Government is contemplating only minor changes to the system in its forthcoming and much postponed Special Educational Needs and Disability Rights in Education Bill.[42] The Special Educational Needs section of this bill:

- proposes that LEAs will be required to establish a statutory Parent Partnership Service for all pupils with Special Educational Needs;

- promises a revision of, rather than a radical alteration to, the *Code of Practice*;

- lays further and more onerous duties on LEAs concerning Statements and the role of the statutory Special Educational Needs Tribunal.

All of these changes are likely to make the new system for dealing with Special Educational Needs more onerous to operate, more bureaucratic and more expensive without correcting any of the fundamental flaws outlined above.

The time has come to rethink the whole subject and to develop a system which is both more realistic in its expectations and more efficient in its workings.

---

42   *Special Educational Needs and Disability Rights in Education Bill: Consultation Document*, DfEE, March 2000; see also *Meeting Special Educational Needs : A programme of action*, DfEE, 1998.

CHAPTER NINE
A CASE STUDY

To give a detailed local example of the current situation in Britain, consider this account of schools – and one school in particular – in the London Borough of Tower Hamlets:

> It is astonishing to discover that there are many primary schools across the country where 40% of the children are registered by their teachers as having Special Educational Needs. In the London Borough of Tower Hamlets, for instance, there are only six schools that have fewer than 20% of children registered with SEN. Twenty-four schools have more than 20% of children with SEN, 18 schools have 30% or more, seven have well over 40%, and one has 55%. Tower Hamlets is not alone in having these astonishing proportions of SEN children. Britain lists far more than other European countries, as the DfEE admits. Clearly, in this country, all too many teachers think that Special Educational Needs are not really special at all, but more or less normal.

> One might argue, and people do, that Tower Hamlets has particular problems – poverty, overcrowding and many children who do not speak English as a first language. However the Government's SEN code of practice specifically says that a child must not be regarded as having a learning difficulty solely because the language of his home is different from the language in which he will be taught.

> And there is no reason to suppose that Tower Hamlets children have more disabilities than other children, or that SEN are genuinely so common. Ruth Miskin is the head teacher of the Kobi Nazrul school in Tower Hamlets, and she, apparently, doesn't believe it either. Most

untypically, she has registered only five pupils (3% of her school) as having SEN. Yet her children are not selected in any way. They come from exactly the same catchment area as the Tower Hamlets schools that have registered 30 to 40% of their children. There is no special selection.

Nearly 80% of the children at Kobi Nazrul are Bangladeshi; English is their second language and some arrive at school hardly speaking any. In 1997, 63% of the pupils qualified for free school meals, a clear indication of poverty. The average class size is 27.5. 70% of the children in the local ward live in overcrowded households, according to the latest census.

Yet these children have consistently done extremely well; they scored above the national average in reading, writing and maths in the recent government tests (SATs). They scored easily the highest in Tower Hamlets in reading tests and got an excellent inspection report from Ofsted. All the seven-year-olds at Kobi Nazrul, without exception, can read.

Ignore SEN and it will go away ?

"Something stands out a mile here: a negligible rate of SEN registration seems to go hand in hand with a very high rate of reading success."

Something stands out a mile here; a negligible rate of SEN registration seems to go with a very high rate of reading success. That is because Ruth Miskin and her staff are passionately interested in literacy – she believes that every healthy child can learn to read – and particularly in a rigorous system of phonics, about which she has lectured and written a great deal. Properly taught, a comprehensive phonics system enables children to learn very fast, with great confidence. This means they avoid the common sense of failure and frustration of poor readers, and the disruptive behaviour that goes with it, which also leads to SEN registration.

Effectively, phonics keeps children off the SEN register. On closer inspection, it emerges that an enormous proportion of SEN children, perhaps as large as three-quarters, are labelled that way simply because they cannot read, or cannot learn to read. That is not because something is wrong with them, there's something wrong with the way they're taught. "Most of what schools see as SEN has to do with illiteracy, and much of it is created by the schools themselves," says Martin Turner. "Most literacy teaching is ineffective and children are being crippled as a result."[43]

More recent data shows that pupils at Kobi Nazrul are below the Tower Hamlets average in the baseline assessments made when they enter the school.

---

43   M Marrin, "The teachers' plot to make our children into failures", *The Daily Telegraph*, 17 December, 1998.

CHAPTER TEN
WHAT MUST BE DONE TO REDUCE THE NUMBERS WITH SEN

The great expansion in the number of pupils deemed to have Special Educational Needs but without Statements is possibly both a cause and a symptom of the substantial under-achievement in many schools.[44]

It could be a cause in that the effort to provide for special needs pupils in ordinary undifferentiated classrooms deflects energies away from the direct teaching of most pupils.

It could be a symptom in that, without the vast apparatus of special needs provision, attention would surely have focused much earlier on the scale of the under-achievement and the consequent need for substantial reform of accepted practices in many schools.

The case for looking for pedagogic causes for the great expansion is particularly strong since there is no comparable growth in Special Educational Needs in other countries except in the USA.[45]

---

44   J Marks, *Standards of English & Maths in Primary Schools for 1995*; *Standards of Reading, Spelling & Maths for 7-year olds in Primary Schools for 1995*; *An Anatomy of Failure: Standards in English Schools for 1997*, Social Market Foundation, 1996, 1997 & 1998.

45   *The Integration of Disabled Children into Mainstream Education: Ambitions, Theories and Practices*, OECD, Paris, 1994 gives percentages for the total number of pupils receiving special educational provision for a wide range of countries – France, Ireland, Italy, Japan, New Zealand, Australia (NSW), Portugal and Spain – in the range of 1% to about 3%;

29

In order to do this, it may be helpful to try to relate the rise in these numbers, with other contemporary changes in education In doing so, it needs to be remembered that changes in practice in education are not reflected in what actually happens to the pupils until considerably later. For example, if a child is not taught to read when he or she is five – in say 1980 – then that child will still be suffering major problems when still at school 11 years later in 1991.

The increase in the number of pupils with SEN can be traced back to the abandonment of traditional teaching methods .

The increase in the number of pupils with Special Educational Needs began in the 1970s and has continued ever since. Over that period the major changes in educational policy and thinking include:

- the perceived need to change the definition of Special Educational Needs in the mid-1970s, as reflected in the pressures which led to the setting up of the Warnock Committee;

- the perception of teachers of the needs of their pupils in the early 1980s as reflected in the research by Croll and Moses published in 1985;[46]

- the changes in primary school practice following on from the Plowden Report in 1967; one key statement was that schools should set out:

  ...to devise the right environment for children, to allow them to be themselves and to develop in the way and at the pace appropriate to them.

- the emergence of the "disorderly classroom" and the related retreat from teaching from the mid- to late-1970s onwards as described and documented by Melanie Phillips in *All Must have Prizes;*[47]

- the retreat from teaching of reading by means of intensive early phonics and its replacement in the late 1970s and early 1980s by the Whole Language or Real Books ideology;[48]

---

the only country with a larger figure – about 10% – is the USA. The paper also lists the 11 defined categories of handicapped children legally recognised in the USA. *Statistical Abstract of Education, Science, Sports and Culture*, Monbusho, Japan, 1996 gives figures for three categories of handicap – blind, deaf and otherwise handicapped – which total less than 1%. *Educational Statistics, 1998*, Swiss Federal Statistical Office, Neuchatel, 1998 shows a total of about 5.5% in special educational programmes -about 4% for Swiss nationals and nearly 12% for foreign students. Germany maintains a highly differentiated system of special schools which serve 3 to 4% of the school population; *Statische Berichte des Bayerischen Landesamt fur Statistik und Datenverarbeitung*, 1999 shows that in Bavaria the figure is 4% and there are schools catering for 11 specific categories of handicap which are rather similar to those for the USA.

[46]   P Croll and D Moses, *One in Five*, Routledge & Kegan Paul, 1985.

[47]   M Phillips, *All Must have Prizes*, Little Brown, 1997.

- the measured fall in reading standards of seven-year-olds throughout the 1980s as documented by Martin Turner in *Sponsored Reading Failure*. and attributed by him to the growth of the ideology of Real Books.[49]

All these events may have some connection with the numbers of pupils who in later years are deemed to have Special Educational Needs.

Many of these tendencies are only now being reversed following the revelation of widespread under-achievement – especially in primary schools – by the first National Curriculum tests in 1995. The results of these tests led directly to the introduction of the pilot National Literacy project in 1996 and the widespread adoption of the nationwide National Literacy Strategy in 1999-2000.

Similar developments have taken place in the United States.

Similar developments have taken place in the United States. The United States is the only other country to have experienced such an explosive growth in the number of those deemed to have Special Educational Needs. It has also experienced the same combination of a retreat from traditional teaching methods (and the consequent disorderly classroom[50]) with the acceptance of the Real Books ideology.[51]

Further confirmation of the problems caused by the abandonment of traditional teaching methods can be found in the accounts of *Effective Methods of Organising Classes within Schools* and *Efficient Teaching Styles and Strategies* which are given in Appendix 1 below.

In summary, these reports of research on teaching in this country and abroad together with estimates of the efficiency of different teaching practices show that:

- dividing pupils into more homogeneous classes, as opposed to mixed-ability teaching groups, can decrease the spread of attainment in individual classes by a factor as large as five;[52]

---

[48]   J Chall, *The Academic Achievement Challenge: What really works in the classroom*, Guilford Press, 2000, pp 58-68 gives an authoritative account of the phonics/whole language controversy.

[49]   M Turner, *Sponsored Reading Failure*, IEA Education Unit, 1990.

[50]   J E Stone, *Developmentalism: An Obscure but Pervasive Restriction on Educational Improvement*, Education Policy Analysis Archives, Vol 4, No 8, April 1996 gives a clear contemporary account of the problems in teacher training in the USA and analyses "developmentalism' – one of the main causes of the retreat from teaching identified so persuasively by Melanie Phillips in schools in this country.

[51]   A Coulson, *Market Education: The Unknown History*, Transaction Publishers, 1999 gives a comprehensive account of the historical development of teacher training in the USA and of the lack of accountability and effectiveness in many schools.

[52]   S Prais, *Grouping and Teaching Efficiency in a Normal School Class*, Discussion Paper No 114, National Institute of Economic and Social Research, 1986.

- emulating in this country the widespread continental practice of more direct whole-class interactive teaching would be highly desirable;[53]

- mixed-ability teaching, so widely advocated from the 1960s onwards, was never very effective and was criticised, in devastating terms, by HMI as long ago as 1978;[54]

- the continental practice of requiring a small number of pupils to repeat a year can improve motivation and learning, and leads to more homogeneous teaching groups which are easier to teach effectively;

- the "good primary practice" of the 1970s and 1980s does not work;[55]

- the efficiency gain of more interactive whole-class teaching may be large – perhaps an improvement by a factor as large as five;[56]

- the combined effects of decreased variability and increased efficiency due to whole-class teaching could therefore lead to an improvement by as much as a factor of 10.

It is striking that most of the points discussed above could be described as supporting the common sense view of what is likely to be effective in schools.

The combined effects of mixed-ability classes and the retreat from direct teaching and from didacticism during the 1970s and 1980s are therefore likely to have been enormous. Equally, the gain in efficiency – year on year during a pupil's schooling – from substantial reform would probably be very large indeed.

This has partly been recognised in the teaching methods set out in the National Literacy Strategy and even more in the National Numeracy Strategy. These will, however, take years to take effect and are just a beginning of what is needed.

But the effects of the retreat from traditional teaching practices have left a disastrous legacy, a legacy which includes, *inter alia*:

- the very large numbers of pupils now designated as having Special Educational Needs;

- the even larger numbers of lower achieving pupils who have been inadequately educated over the last two decades;

- a whole generation of teachers who have not been trained to teach, and who are poorly educated because of the general lowering of expectations in schools and university.

---

53   S J Prais and E Beadle, *Pre-vocational Schooling in Europe Today*, National Institute of Economic and Social Research, 1991.

54   *Mixed Ability Work in Comprehensive Schools*, HMI Series: Matters for Discussion, HMSO, 1978.

55   R Alexander, *Primary Education in Leeds*, University of Leeds, 1991.

56   J Marks, *Value for Money in Education: Opportunity Costs & the Relationship between Standards and Resources*, Campaign for Real Education, June 1992, Chapter 4.

RECOMMENDATIONS

1. Withdraw the *Code of Practice*

The *Code of Practice on the Identification and Assessment of Special Educational Needs* should be withdrawn because it is so imprecise as to be virtually meaningless. Ample experience and evidence have shown that it is unenforceable in practice.

2. Annual monitoring of reading

All special needs pupils should be required to take externally-administered standardised tests of reading and spelling each year in order to focus attention on the needs of the pupil and on the school's effectiveness in meeting them.[57]

The results of these tests should determine whether or not the particular policies – and associated funding – should continue.

If no significant progress in reading has taken place, pupils should be withdrawn from normal classrooms and given specific intensive instruction in reading – by means of an intensive phonics programme for at least one hour a day – either in the school or elsewhere. This should be followed, once a pupil's decoding skills are reasonably satisfactory, by an intensive programme which seeks to make up for the lost ground in language comprehension and vocabulary acquisition.[58]

3. Reforming teaching practices and school organisation

The main priority should not be 'inclusion' – especially if this means more inefficient mixed-ability classes or other wasteful arrangements – but effective provision for all from the start.

The disruption to many schools caused by much current special needs provision could probably be considerably reduced by:

- teaching reading earlier and more effectively;

- more academic selection both within and between schools;

- continuing to discourage mixed-ability teaching and encourage grouping by ability;

- introducing the continental practice of repeating a year (see Appendix 2).

Much can be learnt by the detailed study of successful teaching practices in other countries (this is being done in a long term project in the London

---

[57] See *Pupils with specific learning difficulties in mainstream schools – A survey of the provision in mainstream primary and secondary schools for pupils with a Statement of Special Educational Needs relating to specific learning difficulties*, Ofsted, 1999 which commends (p 12) the annual use of standardised tests of reading comprehension and reading accuracy for pupils with specific learning difficulties (dyslexia). Why not for all pupils with Special Educational Needs with or without Statements?

[58] See A Cunningham & K Stanovich, *What reading does for the mind* in *The Unique Power of Reading and How to Unleash it*, The American Educator, American Federation of Teachers, Spring/Summer, 1998, pp 8-15.

Borough of Barking and Dagenham in collaboration with researchers at the National Institute of Economic and Social Research). By adapting successful teaching methods from Germany and Switzerland which involve much whole-class interactive teaching, the long tail of under-achieving pupils in basic mathematics, who might otherwise be classified as having Special Educational Needs, has been considerably reduced.[59]

CONCLUSION

These changes when fully implemented over a number of years, are likely to reduce substantially the numbers of pupils who are currently designated as having "Special Educational Needs" because these pupils will then have been taught more effectively.

But it will be a slow process. Therefore given the long lead times in education before the effects of reforms can be seen and the long period during which the "Special Educational Needs" explosion took place, the changes recommended here should begin at once.

At the same time an official National Enquiry should be set up which should take evidence from, but not include amongst its members, people with qualifications or employment in Special Educational Needs. The National Enquiry should establish the scale of the present waste of resources, monitor the effects of the changes proposed above for dealing with "Special Educational Needs", and review the provision for real Special Educational Needs, a subject to which we now turn.

---

[59]   J Whitburn, "A Tale of Two Systems, Special Children", *Special Needs*, May, 2000.

CHAPTER ELEVEN
WHAT MUST BE DONE TO HELP THOSE WITH REAL SEN

In education, there is now an overwhelming presumption in favour of "inclusion". This is often taken to mean that all children, regardless of ability or disability or even behaviour, should attend mainstream rather than special schools.[60]

This presumption is threatening to pre-empt the real debate about what is best for pupils and to override both parental wishes and the views of teachers

In fact, many parents actually prefer special schools to mainstream schools; equally many teachers favour inclusion more in theory than in practice. One teachers' union, the NASUWT, opposes it outright.

The case for special schools is also much stronger now than perhaps it was in the early 1980s especially since the development of the National Curriculum. According to a recent report by Ofsted[61], the aspirations of special schools –

---

60 The campaign for full inclusion has been encouraged by international pronouncements such as UNESCO's 1992 Salamanca Statement, which declared that mainstream schools:
> "are the most effective means of combating discriminatory attitudes, creating welcoming communities, building an inclusive society and achieving education for all; moreover they provide an effective education to the majority of children and improve the efficiency and ultimately the cost-effectiveness of the entire education system."

61 *Special Education 1994-98: a review of special schools, secure units & pupil referral units in England*, Ofsted, 1999.

and the expectations they have of their pupils – have been transformed in the 1990s so that the arguments against them which carried weight in earlier decades may now have much less force.

Moreover, the debate is also confused by the rising costs – as outlined in Chapter 5 – of the present system of dealing with Special Educational Needs. Indeed *The Economist* claims that one aim of the government's new bill – the Special Educational Needs and Disability Rights in Education Bill – is to reduce costs by reducing the number of children receiving Statements. The article goes so far as to conclude that:

> ...if the number of children with special needs keeps rising, both the financing and conceivably even the very function of mainstream schooling will be called into question.[62]

The time has come to be radical.

Perhaps the time has come to be radical and to question the whole development of policy in this area since the Warnock Committee's work in the 1970s.

The following questions should be asked:

- has the concept of the individual pupil's Statement of Special Educational Need in its present form outlived its usefulness?

- should the concept of defining specific categories of disability be revived (this was used in the UK and is still used in many other countries)?

Any definitions of disability should first focus on those categories which are easiest to specify with some hope of precision. Categories which are unspecific and thus more difficult to define – examples include Moderate Learning Difficulties, Severe Learning Difficulties and Emotional and Behavioural Difficulties – should be left to later.[63]

---

62   "Making a statement", *The Economist*, 8 January, 2000, p 33.

63   It may be that the growth of pupil numbers in these categories could, to a certain extent, be related to the long history of ineffective early teaching of reading and may substantially decrease if the policies recommended in the previous Chapter are implemented.

CHAPTER TWELVE
CONCLUSIONS

Does the explosion in Special Educational Needs reflect an extraordinary decline in the well-being of so many children? Or is it induced by the failure of schools to teach properly? In particular, would effective methods of teaching children to read – an area in which failure which has been increasingly widely acknowledged – do much to reverse the sharp increase in pupils classified as having SEN.[64]

More data is, of course, needed in the public domain – together with answers to the unanswered questions in Chapter Six. It is extraordinary that so little has been done to shed light on such an important and expensive matter.

t is time to ask whether we have brought this disaster upon ourselves.

But it surely must be time to explore pragmatically and operationally the alternative hypothesis – that we may have brought this disaster on ourselves. If that is the case, then the recommendations in Chapters 10 and 11 should be implemented without delay.

---

[64]   For example, Estelle Morris at a Guardian debate in 1998, when she was criticised for the prescriptive nature of the National Literacy and Numeracy Strategies, accused the teachers present and many other teachers too of a lack of professionalism going back many years. Of course she didn't put it as directly as that. What she said was we now know what works and we owe it to the children to make sure they are taught properly because they only have one chance.

If this hypothesis is correct, then the benefits stretch far beyond those wrongly identified as having SEN. For example, teachers would not have such a wide range of ability to teach in the same class, and could thus teach much more effectively. Pupils, especially the less able, will be better taught – and taught to read in particular. And pupils generally will benefit from the improved and more focused teaching which will be increasingly possible.

It is essential to monitor whether or not special needs pupils can read or not, for the sake of the children themselves, but also to establish some sense of accountability. It is professional negligence of the most culpable kind to provide substantial resources with no sense of whether they are being used effectively.

Existing policies on Special Educational Needs must therefore be scrutinised – in the interests of all those pupils who have over the years been failed by 'the system'.

APPENDIX 1
BETTER TEACHING METHODS[65]

Note: All the examples quoted in this Appendix were published in 1992 or before and therefore relate to practices in the 1980s or earlier – that is to more than a decade ago. Any suspect or ineffective practices that were current then, particularly for primary school pupils, could clearly lead to further problems in the 1990s as pupils pass through the education system. This is just the period when we have seen that the numbers of pupils diagnosed as having Special Educational Needs increased so rapidly.

EFFECTIVE METHODS OF ORGANISING CLASSES WITHIN SCHOOLS

This topic is worth considering separately even though it is clearly related to the question of using effective teaching strategies within a class. This is illustrated by these comments[66] from British teachers concerning continental schools:

> The process of class-repetition combined with a differentiated system of secondary schooling, sometimes combined with further streaming within each type of school, obviously leads to a *very* much narrower range of attainment amongst the pupils in each class facing a teacher: 'it is therefore considerably easier for a German teacher to organise and teach classes'. (T)

---

65   This appendix is based on J Marks, *Value for Money in Education: Opportunity Costs & the Relationship between Standards and Resources*, Campaign for Real Education, June 1992, Chapter 4.

66   S J Prais and E Beadle, *Pre-vocational Schooling in Europe Today*, National Institute of Economic and Social Research, 1991, pp 22-3.

...continental teachers do not rule out that mixed-ability classes can be taught effectively: but the dominant view seems to be that only 'teachers of outstanding ability – perhaps one in a thousand'(T) would be able to do so; equally, 'only one in a hundred pupils' would learn as effectively in a mixed ability class – even when working at his own pace from worksheets or within a small group – as when 'working together as a reasonably homogeneous class led by a teacher'.

(T: Teacher comment)

There is little mixed-ability teaching in Continental comprehensive schools. These schools usually contain separate streams following curricula similar to those offered in the separate academic, technical and vocational schools. Such schools are therefore best described as multilateral rather than comprehensive and can teach in similar ways to the separate kinds of school:

Because Continental classes are relatively homogeneous, a 'graduated' set of 'short-term goals' can be devised for the whole class; as one of our visiting teachers put it: 'pupils are being well educated without being expected to attain unrealistic goals'. In contrast, faced with the problem of teaching a British class spanning virtually the whole range of attainments and abilities, a British teacher needs to devise tasks such that 'the intellectual ability and aspiration of average and higher achievers would be fully stretched' at the same time as those of more modest attainers. This is very difficult: tasks that are too easy leave high-attainers bored and fractious; tasks that are too hard for low-attainers leave them incapacitated and rebellious.[67]

This conclusion is strongly supported by a detailed HMI report on mixed ability teaching in secondary schools published as long ago as 1978.[68] This report concluded that:

In most of the schools visited...HMI felt concern about the level, pace and scope of the work in a significant number of subjects. This concern was sometimes on behalf of pupils of all abilities; more frequently it related to the extremes of the ability range; most frequently it related to the most able pupils.

....abler pupils sometimes underachieved in order to conform to the level of their class-mates.

...often, the most able pupils were insufficiently extended because their teachers did not realise what they were capable of achieving. A not inconsiderable number of teachers had no experience of the

---

67   Ibid., p 24.

68   *Mixed Ability Work in Comprehensive Schools*, HMI Series: Matters for Discussion, HMSO, 1978.

level and quality of work that can be achieved by able pupils in streamed or setted groups, and found it difficult to appreciate their potential and meet their needs when they encountered them as individuals or as a small minority in a mixed group.

HMI also found that mixed ability teaching was more demanding both of the time and the skill of a teacher:

Preparations for teaching mixed ability groups demands substantially more of a teacher's time than preparation for teaching more homogeneous groups.

Catering adequately for the full ability range within each mixed ability group calls for more sophisticated professional skills than does teaching in more traditional forms of organisation.

...success was achieved by teachers of strong commitment and exceptional skill. Teachers of average ability found great difficulty in meeting the complex requirements of teaching mixed ability groups.

...in the hands of the average teacher...the mixed ability class tended to function at the level of the average pupil. For the weaker teacher, the challenge of the mixed ability class was simply too great.

In summary, for most teachers and pupils – perhaps the overwhelming majority – mixed ability teaching does not work.

It therefore seems that there is much to be gained, both for pupils and for teachers, from abandoning mixed ability teaching and using more homogeneous teaching groups wherever possible.

As the Channel Four Commission on Education concluded as long ago as 1991:

...with a narrower spread of pupil attainments, it will become easier for the teacher to spend a greater portion of each school period teaching the class as a whole, rather than breaking each class into groups working at different levels. This should make it easier to maintain systematic teaching. We also recommend that teachers modify their teaching styles to promote a more ordered teaching environment as observed in continental schools.[69]

EFFICIENT TEACHING STYLES AND STRATEGIES.

Research by Professor Robin Alexander into primary schools in Leeds in the 1980s gives a graphic picture of what was regarded as "good primary practice" at that time.[70]

His report noted that a sizeable minority of primary school teachers:

---

[69]   *Every Child in Britain*, Report of the Channel Four Commission on Education, 1991, p 28.
[70]   R Alexander, *Primary Education in Leeds*, University of Leeds, 1991.

...appeared to undertake little written planning and to leave more than was defensible to the last minute. Such a response to the demands of teaching was sometimes defended on the grounds of 'flexibility', and indeed there is still a body of opinion in primary education which sees written planning as by definition the product of inflexible thinking and practice. However, the failure to engage in forward planning seemed to reflect anything but favourably on the commitment and capacities of some of the teachers concerned, and reinforces our view that 'flexibility' is a much abused word in primary education.

Such influential attitudes must make it difficult for teachers to teach effectively and for pupils to learn especially when a local education authority is bent on imposing its own version of 'good primary practice' on schools. In Leeds this involved three prominent and recurrent requirements:

(i)   to have children working in groups;
In other words whole class teaching was strongly discouraged. This often meant that teachers focused attention primarily on those children who demanded it. As Professor Alexander noted:

> The price that some children pay for demanding little of the teacher may be that they are given work which demands little of them.

(ii) to have the different groups pursuing different areas of the curriculum at any one time;
Professor Alexander observed that:

> ...only thus can the goal of 'seamlessness' in curriculum and learning be achieved. For some teachers not only was this difficult to plan and implement as an organisational strategy *per se*, but the increased demands imposed on them by the strategy meant that their opportunities for systematic and sustained monitoring of children's progress were further reduced, while at the same time the increased levels of movement and disturbance in the classroom might adversely affect children's concentration and time on task.

(iii) to adopt a predominantly 'enquiry' or 'exploratory' mode of teacher-pupil interaction and to couple this with plenty of encouragement and support for children's responses.
Again Professor Alexander commented that:

> In keeping with the taboo on didacticism which has been a strong feature of post-Plowden primary education in this country, teachers generally preferred to ask questions rather than make statements or give direct instructions.

> [Even] where a simple clear statement would have saved a great deal of time...there was a reluctance to say openly that a particular

answer to a question was wrong. Incorrect answers were sometimes ignored; more often they were praised as if they were right, and then ignored. Conversely, correct answers were sometimes treated as if they were incorrect.

> ...the unthinking and undiscriminating use of questions...may reflect...a 'taboo on didacticism', a sense that children at all costs must not be told. The result...can be a charade of pseudo-enquiry which fools nobody, least of all the children, but which wastes a great deal of time. Similarly, the indiscriminate and thus unhelpful use of praise...may stem from a laudable concern that children be encouraged and supported in their learning. Yet in the end this too can be counterproductive, with children becoming confused or cynical in the face of what they may begin to see as so much mere noise.

Such uncertainties were reinforced by the local authority's insistence on what they perceived to be the correct classroom layout.

> ...a thematically-dominated integrated curriculum is best achieved through an 'integrated' arrangement of furniture.

> The layout commended...as less a suggestion than a requirement, work bays for each major area of the curriculum. These were intended to facilitate patterns of curriculum provision generally denoted by terms like the 'flexible day' or 'integrated day', in which at any one time a classroom will contain children working on quite disparate tasks in different areas of the curriculum. Since some such tasks might involve children standing or working on the floor, advisory staff also encouraged teachers to make flexible use of furniture, some commending what was termed the concept of 'fewer chairs than children': the argument being that since the nature of the activity did not require one chair per child, more space for those activities could be created by dispensing with superfluous chairs.

Professor Alexander concluded:

> The classroom arrangements and curriculum patterns recommended, though arguable in terms of progressive ideology, have come in for increasing criticism as to their capacity to promote children's concentration and learning, and the effective management, interaction, diagnosis and assessment on which learning and progress depend.

> Despite the well-documented evidence of this kind, such arrangements continued to be commended as constituting 'good primary practice'.

There is a clear contrast between what was regarded in the 1970s and 1980s as 'good primary practice' in Britain and the teaching methods that HMI warmly commended in 1991 in a report on French primary schools.[71] In French lessons in France:

> The pace of the lessons seen was, almost without exception, brisk and demanding of a high level of concentration.

> ...in the best lessons a confident progress through quite long periods of time – up to forty five minutes at a stretch even with the youngest children – indicated that teachers had developed from their training and from teaching manuals the ability to sequence activities. This gave the children sufficient practice at different tasks to achieve success.

> ...the teacher often taught the class in one group...and...engaged children in question and answer sessions, during which almost all the pupils in the class were given the opportunity to answer.

> ...the standards of work achieved by nearly all the children were good and sometimes very good.

> ...in all the lessons the teacher continually checked that learning was taking place by asking questions and checking the work.

In mathematics:

> ...similar tasks were given to the whole class at the same time. Each lesson always included a well-defined beginning and a sequence of small steps towards a pre-determined goal. Exposition by the teacher alternated with tasks of relatively short duration which enabled the children to practise what they had heard explained at each stage.

> Whole-class teaching and close direction of lessons by the teacher resulted in some significant gains. The level of teacher expectation was high, the activities proceeded at a brisk pace, and there was usually a clear progression within the lessons themselves. The quality of exposition and the use of questioning by the teachers were invariably very good, enabling them to hold the attention of most of the class for long periods at a time.

---

71   *Aspects of Primary Education in France*, HMI, 1991.

APPENDIX 2
ACADEMIC OR SOCIAL PROMOTION?

The policy of grouping children into classes according to their academic achievement as opposed to their age has its origins in the Jesuit schools in the 16th Century. They divided their secondary curriculum into five grades:

> Rather than grouping children by age as is commonly done today, they were grouped according to their grasp of the course materials.[72]

The resulting increase in efficiency of instruction was one reason for the very rapid growth of Jesuit schools and their imitators over the next century.

The main aim of the policy is to ensure that teachers are teaching a group that is reasonably homogeneous in academic attainment. This raises standards by facilitating the more efficient practice of whole-class teaching rather trying to teach pupils individually or in small groups. In this, it is a continuation and extension of the policy of grouping pupils by ability and attainment within a year group.

Normally most pupils advance from year to year with their age group but this is not automatic. The decision to advance a child is usually taken by the teacher based on the work done over the school year, possibly including results on tests and internal school examinations, but with considerable discussion with pupils and parents; pupils usually have to show reasonable achievement across a range of subjects.

---

72 A Coulson, *Market Education: The Unknown History*, Transaction Publishers, 1999, p 69.

An important secondary benefit is that the possibility of being held back a year – which is usually mooted relatively early in the year with parents being informed – can have a stimulating effect on the work rate of pupils.

In principle, it has much in common with setting or streaming or selection in that the aim is to teach pupils of all levels of attainment more effectively and at a faster pace by having pupils of similar attainment together.

The practice is widespread on the continent – in Germany, Austria, Switzerland, the Netherlands and France, for example – and is largely accepted there; moreover, it is not uncommon in independent schools in this country. It is currently being mooted in some states in the United States.[73]

Relatively few continental pupils repeat a year a second time but a fairly high proportion – say 30 to 40% – may repeat a year at some time in their school career. The highest figures for repeating a year are in France; on a SCAA visit there in 1994 we were told that by the end of Primary (11) 33% had repeated a year and 8% had repeated twice; by the end of Lower Secondary (16) 43% had repeated a year; and 15 to 20% repeated the first year of the baccalaureate. In other countries the figures are considerably lower.

One particularly effective way in which the policy is used is in some parts of Germany where those pupils for whom German is not their first language are expected to reach a reasonable standard in German at the start of their schooling before they enter the usual school system at 6; if they don't qualify, a special year's preparatory schooling is provided.

73   *Fail the test, miss the grade*, The Economist, 10 April 1999.

RECENT POINTMAKERS FROM THE CENTRE FOR POLICY STUDIES

THE BAD SAMARITAN: the War of Independence Part II £10.00
Maurice Saatchi and Peter Warburton

The authors declare 'Independence Day', the day on which people stop working for Government and start working for themselves. In 2000, Independence Day falls on 30 May. Three years ago it fell 5 days earlier, on May 25. The problem is the massive overlap between the tax and benefit payments. A once in a lifetime opportunity may have arisen to simplify the tax system. For the Chancellor of the Exchequer has not only collected a £22.5 billion bonanza from the auction of mobile phone licences. He is also the recipient of a second, just as unexpected but even more lucrative stream of revenue, one which, in the last fiscal year alone, was worth £14 billion. The UK is reaping a "Financial Markets Dividend". The income from this Dividend is extremely capricious. If the financial markets decline, it could easily evaporate. Yet the Chancellor's spending commitments are based on the assumption that the Dividend will continue indefinitely. A far better use for the Dividend would be a thorough, one-off, reform of the tax and benefits system.

> *Today is the first day of the year 2000 when average British taxpayers starts working for themselves rather than for the Government. Tax freedom day, calculated by the Centre for Policy Studies, has been put back five days in the past three years, because of the growing tax burden – The Times*

THE GREAT AND GOOD? The rise of the New Class £7.50
Martin McElwee

A new establishment has been surreptitiously levered into key positions of power in Britain. A large number of New Labour supporters from the worlds of the media, showbusiness, the arts, business, the law and academia have been drafted in to take a plethora of jobs at the heart of our polity. Its effects are insidious and include the undermining of the neutrality of the civil service, the marginalisation of the House of Commons and the politicisation of private life to an unprecedented degree – all inspired by a faith in the efficacy of social engineering.

> *In a pamphlet that will prove hugely influential, Martin McElwee lays bare some of the reality that lies behind Mr Blair's government. His findings are, in some cases, devastating. **His pamphlet should be read by everyone who takes an intelligent interest in British politics** – Peter Oborne in The Express*

HANDICAP, NOT TRUMP CARD £5.00
Keith Marsden

> *"I have just been looking at a detailed survey to be published by the Centre for Policy Studies which shows that the Franco-German model has failed on all counts... It aimed to cut unemployment by increasing state expenditure, legally lowering the number of hours worked each week, instituting compulsory training programmes and initiating early retirement, raising taxes, increasing public investment, imposing collective wages agreements, forcing women into jobs, harmonising workplace health and safety regulations and lowering interest rates. These ten policies, individually and collectively, have brought nothing but disaster." – Paul Johnson in the Daily Mail*

A Subscription to the Centre for Policy Studies

The Centre for Policy Studies runs an Associate Membership Scheme which is available at £55.00 per year (or £50.00 if paid by bankers' order). Associates are entitled to all CPS Pointmakers and pamphlets produced in a 12-month period (of which there at least eighteen); previous publications at *half* their published price; and (whenever possible) reduced fees for the conferences which the Centre holds.

For more details please write or telephone to:
The Secretary
Centre for Policy Studies
57 Tufton Street, London SW1P 3QL
Tel: 020 7222 4488   Fax: 020 7222 4388
e-mail: mail@cps.org.uk   Website: www.cps.org.uk